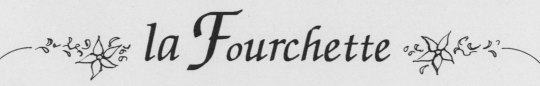

la Fourchette

COMFORT FOOD COOKBOOK

Written by: Lynne K. Pettinger

Illustrated by: Gary Kingman

My Love and Appreciation

To Lucia DiGiovanni and Yeng Sam, my loyal staff at La Fourchette for their constant support; to Margo Bates for her advice and gentle pushing; Trudy Vandop for editing and her incredible support; Sheila Browning for hours at the computer; Kasey Wilson, an expert in the Cookbook field, for giving me the confidence that I needed; to the men at Doppler Computer Center, David Chalk, Ed Thwaites and Mark Dobres who really thought I was going to move in; to Gary Kingman, my friend and illustrator; to Nancy Foreman, for being there; to my family who believed it could happen.

Copyright 1991
Canadian Cataloguing in Publication Data
Pettinger, Lynne
La Fourchette, Comfort Food Cookbook
INCLUDES INDEX.
ISBN 0-9695694-0-8
Printed in Canada

Ten years ago my goal, to own and manage a small restaurant and catering company, was realized. I wanted a place where people could come and feel at home. In my "Pink House" I believe this has been accomplished. My customers walk in and exclaim, "this feels and smells just like Mom's kitchen", a higher compliment I couldn't be paid.

In celebration of La Fourchette's 10th Anniversary, I have written the "Comfort Food Cookbook", comprised of recipes that are used daily in my restaurant; food that brings back memories to all of us.

DEDICATION...

To the most important women in my life:

My mother,
 Mrs. Evalyne Cyr
- my guiding light

My sister,
 Commodore Laraine F. Orthlieb
- my great role model

My daughter,
 Karen Laraine Pettinger
- my inspiration

CONTENTS

Fin

The homemade red
wine is good for
drinking or cooking
OR
best of all its good
for drinking while
your cooking!

I. FINGER TIDBITS

ANTIPASTO

1/2 cup	olive oil
1 med.	cauliflower chopped
26 oz.	pitted black olives drained and chopped
26 oz.	stuffed olives drained and chopped
16 oz.	pickled onions drained and chopped
12 oz. can	mushroom stems & pieces drained
2 lge.	green peppers diced
32 oz.	sweet pickles drained and chopped
4 cups	HOT ketchup
4 oz can	anchovies drained, rinsed and chopped
2-7 1/2 oz.	cans tuna drained, rinsed and flaked
1 lb.	fresh cooked shrimp
1 cup	vinegar

In large pot COMBINE olive oil, cauliflower, black olives, stuffed olives and onions. Bring to a BOIL over high heat. LOWER heat and simmer for 10 minutes. ADD mushrooms, green pepper, pickles, HOT ketchup, anchovies, tuna, shrimp and vinegar. MIX well. BOIL 1 minute. PLACE in sterilized containers and freeze.

HOT CHICKEN WINGS

3 lbs.	chicken wings
1/2 cup	sugar
3 tbsp.	cornstarch
1/2 tsp.	salt
1/2 tsp.	garlic powder
2/3 tsp.	ground ginger
2/3 cup	water
2 tbsp.	tabasco
2 tbsp.	ketchup
2 tsp.	vinegar

Place chicken wings (with tip joints discarded) on oiled baking sheet. BAKE at 350 degrees for 10 minutes.

Combine in saucepan remaining ingredients. Cook stirring constantly over medium heat until thick. Brush over chicken wings and BAKE 10 minutes more. Turn over chicken wings. Brush again with sauce and bake 10 minutes more. PLACE on serving tray.

Yield: 4 - 6 servings

CHILI CHEDDAR CHEESECAKE

1 cup	fine bread crumbs
1 1/2 lbs.	cream cheese
3/4 lb .	medium cheddar grated
1 cup	cottage cheese
3/4 cup	chopped green onion
4	eggs
3 tbsp.	canned chopped jalapeno peppers
6 ozs.	cooked ham diced
2 tbsp.	milk
1 tsp.	chopped garlic

PRESS bread crumbs into 9" springform pan. BEAT cream cheese until smooth. ADD remaining ingredients to cream cheese and MIX thoroughly. POUR into pan and BAKE at 350 degrees for 1 1/4 hours. TURN OFF oven and let sit in oven for 1 hour more. REMOVE from pan.

DECORATE top with tomato rose and chopped jalapenos. SERVE warm with champagne crackers.

GLAZED BRIE

1/2 cup	almonds
1/4 cup	pecans
1/4 cup	walnuts
1/2 tsp.	cinnamon
1/4 tsp.	ginger
1/8 tsp.	nutmeg
1/8 tsp.	allspice
3/4 cup	brown sugar
3 tbsp.	water
1-12"	round brie

PLACE nuts, spices and sugar in food processor. PROCESS until nuts are finely ground. ADD water and process 30 seconds or until mixture holds together. SPREAD evenly on top of brie. BROIL 6" from heat until topping is lightly browned, about 4 minutes. WATCH IT CLOSELY.

DECORATE with apple slices, grapes, and figs. SERVE with crackers.

(DIP apple slices in lemon juice to prevent discoloration)

HOT PEPPER PECANS

3 tbsp.	margarine
2 tsp.	worchestershire sauce
1/4 tsp.	Tabasco
1/4 tsp.	pepper
2 cups	whole pecans

MELT margarine. Over medium heat STIR in worcestershire sauce, Tabasco and pepper. MIX in pecans. SPREAD in shallow baking dish. BAKE 300 degrees 20 minutes STIRRING often. SERVE warm.

Yield: 4 servings

LION SHRIMP

1/4 cup	soya sauce
1 tbsp.	brown sugar
1 tsp.	minced fresh ginger
1 tsp.	minced garlic
10	uncooked large shrimp
1/4 lb.	chicken livers
10 slices	bacon
3 tbsp.	chopped green onion
10	4" bamboo skewers

COMBINE soya sauce, sugar, and ginger in shallow pan. ADD shrimp (peeled and butterflied) and chicken livers (cut in 1" x 1 1/2" strips). COVER and refrigerate for 3 hours. LINE baking sheet with foil. ARRANGE bacon on baking sheet. DRAIN shrimp and chicken livers, reserving marinade. PLACE one shrimp at end of bacon. PLACE one chicken liver strip on top of shrimp. ROLL up lightly completely covering shrimp and chicken liver. PUSH skewer through wide end of shrimp. DRIZZLE with reserved marinade. BROIL 6 inches from heat until bacon sizzles, about 5 minutes, on each side. TRANSFER to platter, SPRINKLE with chopped green onions.

"WONDERFUL"

MUSHROOM STRUDEL

1 envelope	flaky pie crust mix
2 slices	bacon diced
8 oz.	mushrooms chopped
1 medium	onion chopped
4 oz.	cream cheese
1	egg yolk beaten

PREPARE pastry according to package directions. SAUTE bacon until tender. ADD mushrooms and onion. COOK until dry. STIR in cheese. MIX until smooth. DIVIDE pastry in half. ROLL each piece 14" x 5 ". SPREAD 1/2 filling over each piece of pastry. ROLL up jelly roll fashion from long side. PLACE seam side down on ungreased baking sheet. BRUSH with egg yolk. SLASH top. BAKE 350 degrees 20-25 minutes or until golden. CUT into 1/2" slices. SERVE warm.

Yield: 4 - 6 servings

PARTY MEATBALLS

2 lbs.	ground beef
2/3 cup	milk
2	eggs
l/2 cup	grated onion
2 cups	fine bread crumbs
l tsp.	salt
l tsp.	allspice
l tsp.	pepper
3 tbsp.	margarine
3 tbsp.	flour
1 1/2 cups	water
l cup	sour cream
2 tbsp.	ketchup
2 tbsp.	dill weed

COMBINE ground beef, milk, eggs, onion, breadcrumbs, seasonings. MIX lightly. FORM 60 balls. PLACE in baking pan. BAKE 350 degrees l5 minutes. TURN meatballs over. BAKE 10 minutes more. In saucepan MELT margarine. STIR in flour until well mixed. ADD water gradually. COOK until slightly thick stirring constantly. ADD sour cream, ketchup and dill weed. HEAT thoroughly. PLACE meatballs in serving dish. COVER with sauce. SERVE with toothpicks.

Yield: 8 - 10 servings

SAUSAGE ROLLS

1 envelope	flaky pie crust mix
1 lb.	pork sausages
	Dijon mustard
	Basil leaves
	Milk

PREPARE pastry according to package instructions. PARBOIL sausages 5 minutes. COOL. CUT in 1/2" pieces. ROLL out pastry in a square. CUT in 3" squares. SPREAD a little Dijon mustard down the center. SPRINKLE on basil leaves. PLACE sausage at end. ROLL up. PLACE seam side down on ungreased cookie sheet. BRUSH tops with milk. BAKE 400 degrees 20 minutes or until golden. SERVE warm.

Yield: 2 1/2 dozen.

SHRIMP AND WATERCHESTNUTS

1 can	waterchestnuts
1 can	baby shrimp
	mayonnaise

DRAIN waterchestnuts. SLICE each waterchestnut in half. PLACE a dab of mayonnaise on each. TOP with a shrimp.

"FAST, EASY AND ADDICTING"

SMOKED SALMON PATE

1 lb.	smoked salmon
1 lb.	cream cheese
1/2 cup	chopped Spanish onion
3 tbsp.	lemon juice
1/2 tsp.	dill weed.

SKIN and BONE salmon. PLACE all ingredients in food processor or blender and process until smooth. FILL pate mould or crock.

GARNISH with capers, small thin onion slices and lemon wedges.

SERVE with crackers, french bread or Hovis bread.

Yield: 4 - 6 servings

WARM BEAN DIP

1 tbsp.	oil
1 clove	garlic minced
1 med.	onion finely chopped
19 oz. can	red kidney beans drained
2 med.	tomatoes chopped
1 tbsp.	canned jalapeno peppers chopped
1 1/2 cups	grated cheddar cheese
1 tbsp.	fresh cilantro chopped
	Tortilla chips
	sliced raw vegetables

HEAT oil in skillet. ADD garlic and onion. COOK until tender. STIR in beans, tomatoes and jalapeno peppers. COOK until heated through stirring occasionally. With a fork MASH the beans. PLACE in oiled baking dish. SPRINKLE with the cheese. BAKE 325 degrees 10 minutes. SPRINKLE with cilantro. SERVE with Tortilla chips and raw vegetables.

Yield: 6 - 8 servings

la Fourchette

Soup
&
Sandwiches

II. SOUP & SANDWICHES

CREAM OF BROCCOLI SOUP

3 tbsp.	margarine
1 medium	onion chopped
2 stalks	celery diced
2 lbs.	fresh broccoli chopped
4 cups	chicken broth
3 tbsp.	flour
3 tbsp.	water
2 tsp.	nutmeg
	salt and pepper to taste

MELT margarine in pot. ADD onions, celery and broccoli. COOK over medium heat 5 minutes. ADD chicken broth and COOK until tender. PROCESS in food processor or blender until smooth. RETURN to pot. DISSOLVE flour in water and BLEND into broccoli along with milk. ADD nutmeg. Salt and pepper to taste. HEAT gently. SERVE topped with croutons.

Yield: 6 servings

CREAM OF CARROT

2 lbs	carrots peeled and sliced
6 tbsp.	margarine
1 medium	onion chopped
8 cups	chicken broth or 8 cups of water + 2 chicken bouillon cubes
1 cup	milk
2 tsp.	nutmeg
	salt and pepper to taste

MELT margarine in pot. ADD carrots and onions. COOK 5 minutes. ADD chicken broth. COOK until tender. PROCESS in food processor or blender until smooth. RETURN to pot. ADD milk, nutmeg, salt and pepper to taste. HEAT gently.

Yield: 6 servings

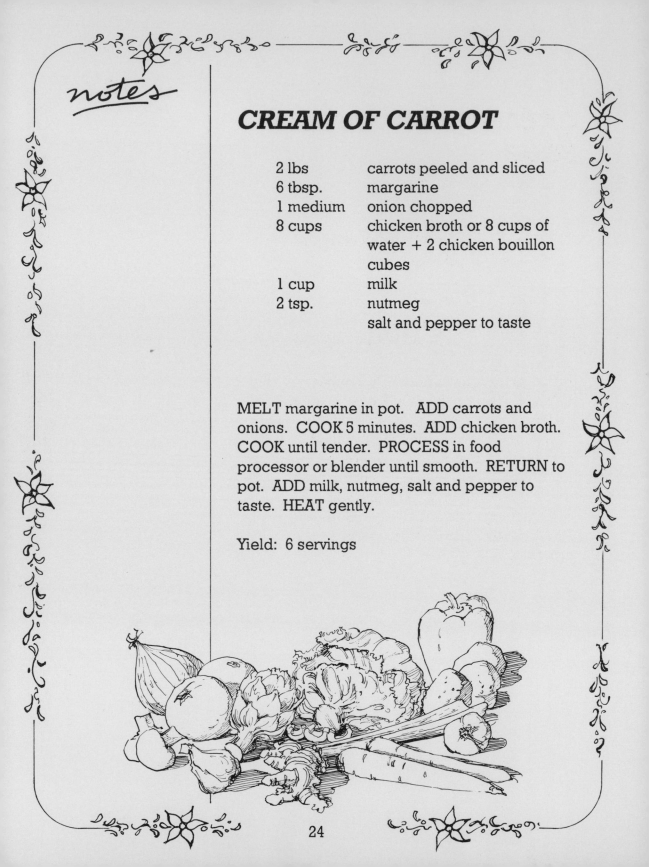

CLAM CHOWDER

3 tbsp.	margarine
2 cups	potatoes, peeled and diced
1 medium	onion, chopped
4 stalks	celery diced
2 tbsp.	flour
2 - 7 oz. cans baby clams
3 cups	milk
	salt and pepper to taste

MELT margarine in pot.   ADD potatoes, onion and celery. SAUTE until tender. BLEND in flour. ADD clams and milk.   Salt and pepper to taste. HEAT gently, stirring often.

YIELD 6 servings.

CORN CHOWDER

3 tbsp.	margarine
3 cups	peeled diced potatoes
1 med.	onion chopped
4 stalks	celery diced
3 tbsp.	flour
4 cups	milk
16 oz.	cream corn
2 tsp.	basil
	salt and pepper

MELT margarine in pot.   ADD potatoes, onion, and celery. SAUTE until tender. BLEND in flour. ADD milk, corn and basil. Salt and pepper to taste. SIMMER over low heat until thoroughly heated.

YIELD 6 servings.

CREAM OF MUSHROOM

4 tbsp.	margarine
1/2 lb.	fresh mushrooms sliced
1 med.	onion diced fine
2	celery stalks, diced fine
1/4 cup	flour
1 tsp.	nutmeg
4 cups	milk

MELT margarine in pot. ADD mushrooms, onions, and celery. COOK until tender. BLEND in flour with nutmeg. ADD milk gradually. SIMMER over low heat stirring often until heated through.

YIELD 6 servings.

notes

POTATO LEEK

3 tbsp.	margarine
4	leeks sliced thin
5	potatoes peeled and diced
4	celery stalks diced
4 tbsp.	flour
4 cups	chicken broth
2 tsp.	tarragon
	salt and pepper

MELT margarine in pot. ADD leeks, potatoes, and celery. SAUTE until tender. BLEND in flour. ADD chicken broth. SIMMER until heated through. ADD tarragon, salt and pepper to taste.

YIELD 6 servings.

13 BEAN SOUP, SOUR CREAM, CILANTRO & SALSA

16 oz. pkg.	13 bean soup mix
1 med.	onion chopped
3 stalks	celery diced
1 1/2 cups	carrots diced
1	green pepper diced
8 cups	chicken stock
1 tsp.	cumin
1 tsp.	garlic powder
1 tsp.	oregano
1 tsp.	chili powder
1 tsp.	salt
1 tsp.	pepper
	fresh cilantro chopped
	sour cream
	salsa

In pot COVER beans with water and COOK until tender. DRAIN and RINSE well. In same pot SAUTE onion, celery, carrots and green pepper until tender. ADD beans, chicken stock and seasonings. HEAT thoroughly.

TOP each serving with a dollop of sour cream, salsa and a sprinkle of cilantro.

Yield: 6 servings

BARLEY BEEF SOUP

3 tbsp.	oil
1 lb.	cubed beef
1 large	onion chopped
2 medium	carrots chopped
3 stalks	celery chopped
1 cup	pearl barley
3 cups	beef broth
1 cup	water
1 tsp.	garlic powder
3 tsp.	basil
	salt and pepper to taste

In pot BROWN beef in oil. ADD onions, carrots celery and barley. COOK over low heat until carrots are tender stirring often. ADD beef broth, water, garlic powder and basil. BRING to a boil. LOWER heat and simmer 30 - 45 minutes stirring often. Salt and pepper to taste.

Yield: 6 servings

HAM AND PEA SOUP

3 tbsp.	margarine
1 medium	onion chopped
4 stalks	celery diced
2	carrots diced
2 cups	split green peas
4 cups	chicken broth
1 cup	diced cooked ham
1 tsp.	thyme
1	bay leaf
	salt and pepper to taste

In pot MELT margarine. ADD onion, celery, carrots and split peas. COOK 5 minutes. ADD chicken broth, ham and seasonings. BRING to a boil. LOWER heat. SIMMER 45 minutes stirring often.

If the soup thickens too much, add more water or chicken broth until it is of the consistency that you prefer.

Yield: 6 servings

CHICKEN NOODLE SOUP

3 tbsp.	margarine
1 medium	onion chopped
3	carrots chopped
3 stalks	celery diced
6 cups	chicken broth
2 cups	cooked diced chicken
3 tsp.	tarragon
8 oz. pkg.	medium noodles
	salt and pepper to taste

In pot MELT margarine. ADD onions, carrots and celery. COOK until tender. ADD chicken broth and tarragon. BRING to a boil. LOWER heat and ADD noodles, salt and pepper. SIMMER 15 minutes.

Yield: 8 servings

ITALIAN SAUSAGE AND BEAN SOUP

1 lb.	dried white beans
1 lb.	ground Italian sausage
2 large	onions chopped
2 cloves	garlic chopped
3 stalks	celery chopped
3 medium	carrots chopped
6 medium	tomatoes chopped
6 cups	beef broth
2 tsp.	oregano
2 tsp.	basil

COVER beans with water and cook until tender. DRAIN and rinse. In pot BROWN sausage meat. ADD onions, garlic, celery, carrots, tomatoes, beans, beef broth and seasonings. BRING to boil. LOWER heat and simmer 30 minutes.

Yield: 6-8 servings.

SHRIMP SALAD SANDWICHES

16 oz.	fresh shrimp, cooked and peeled
1/2 medium	cucumber, peeled, seeded and diced
1 tsp.	dill weed
	mayonnaise
	salt and pepper to taste

MIX shrimp, cucumber, dill weed, salt and pepper. ADD enough mayonnaise to hold together, approx. 1 cup. Yield: 4 sandwiches.

CHICKEN SALAD SANDWICHES

4 cups	cooked chicken, diced
4 stalks	celery, chopped
3 tsp.	chopped parsley
2 medium	tomatoes, chopped
	mayonnaise
	salt and pepper to taste

MIX chicken, celery, parsley, tomatoes, salt and pepper to taste. ADD enough mayonnaise to hold together, approx. 1 1/2 cups.

Yield: 6 sandwiches

EGG SALAD

6	eggs grated
2	green onions chopped
2 tsp.	chopped parsley
2 stalks	celery diced
1 tbsp.	dijon mustard
	mayonnaise
	salt & pepper to taste

BLEND eggs, onion, parsley, celery, mustard, salt and pepper together. ADD enough mayonnaise to hold together, approx. 1/2 cup.

TUNA SALAD

7 oz. can	tuna
2 stalks	celery diced
3 tsp.	chopped parsley
1 tsp.	curry powder*
	mayonnaise
	salt and pepper

DRAIN, RINSE and FLAKE tuna. ADD celery, parsley, curry powder, salt and pepper. MIX in enough mayonnaise to hold together, approx. 1 cup.

YIELD: 4 sandwiches.

*Can be omitted

TURKEY SANDWICHES

1 lb.	sliced roasted turkey meat
8 oz.	cranberry sauce
	stuffing
	mayonnaise

STUFFING:

1/2 cup	margarine
2 lge.	onions chopped
4 stalks	celery chopped
3 tbsp.	poultry seasoning
1/2 cup	water
4 cups	fine bread crumbs
	salt and pepper

STUFFING: MELT margarine, ADD onions and celery. COOK until tender. MIX in seasoning, water, and bread crumbs. Stuffing should be moist and hold together (ADD more water if necessary). Salt and pepper to taste. PACK into loaf pan. BAKE 350 degrees for 30 minutes.

ASSEMBLY: 8 slices of bread. SPREAD each slice of bread with butter and mayonnaise. On 4 slices place 4 oz. each of stuffing and turkey, 1 oz. of cranberry sauce, lettuce or sprouts, salt and pepper to taste.

YIELD 4 sandwiches.

la Fourchette

Salads
&
Salad Dressings

III. SALADS AND SALAD DRESSINGS

MARINATED VEGETABLE SALAD

1 cup	chopped broccoli
1 cup	chopped cauliflower
1 cup	chopped zucchini
1 cup	peeled and diced carrots

DRESSING:

2-1/2 cups	vegetable oil
1 cup	vinegar
1/2 cup	grated parmesan
1/2 tbsp.	brown sugar
1 tbsp.	salt
1/2 tbsp.	celery salt
1 tsp.	pepper
1 tsp.	dry mustard
1 tsp.	paprika

PLACE all dressing ingredients in a jar and shake well. TOSS vegetables together. MIX in 1 cup dressing.

Dressing will keep 4 weeks in refrigerator.

Yield: 4 servings

PASTA SALAD

2 cups	rotini pasta cooked drained and rinsed.

DRESSING:

1/2 cup	mayonnaise
1/2 cup	cream cheese
1/4 cup	red wine vinegar
1/2 tsp.	Dijon mustard
2 tsp.	dill weed
1 clove	garlic minced
1 tbsp.	basil
1 tbsp.	lemon juice

WHISK dressing ingredients together until smooth.

TO DRESSING ADD:

1/2 cup	chopped broccoli
1/2 cup	diced zucchini
1 cup	cooked shrimp

TOSS dressing with pasta. Refrigerate.

YIELD 6 servings.

POTATO SALAD

6 med.	potatoes cooked, peeled and diced
1/2 cup	celery diced
1/2 cup	grated carrots
1	green onion sliced
3	hard boiled eggs chopped
1 cup	sweet salad dressing
	salt and pepper to taste

TOSS all above ingredients together. MIX in sweet salad dresing.

SWEET SALAD DRESSING

1 cup	sugar
1 tsp.	salt
1/2 tbsp.	dry mustard
2 tbsp.	flour
2	eggs
1/2 tsp.	tumeric
1 can	Eagle Brand condensed milk
1/2 cup	vinegar
1 litre	mayonnaise

BEAT sugar, salt, dry mustard, flour, eggs, and tumeric together until slightly thick. ADD condensed milk, vinegar and mayonnaise. BEAT together for 3 minutes.

Yield: 6 servings

The remainder of the Sweet Salad Dressing will keep 4 weeks refrigerated.

notes

CHICKEN SALAD WITH POPPYSEED DRESSING

4 cups	butter lettuce leaves
4 cups	washed spinach leaves
2 tbsp. each	margarine and oil
4 boned and	skinned chicken breasts
1/4 cup	flour
1 tsp. each	salt and pepper

POPPYSEED DRESSING:

1	egg
1/8 cup	sugar
1 tbsp.	Dijon mustard
2/3 cup	red wine vinegar
3 tsp.	grated onion
2 cups	vegetable oil
3 tbsp.	whole poppyseeds

PLACE egg, sugar, Dijon mustard, red wine vinegar, onion in food processor or blender. PROCESS 30 seconds. With motor running gradually ADD oil. STIR in poppyseeds.

MIX flour, salt and pepper together. DREDGE chicken in flour mixture. MELT margarine, ADD oil. BROWN chicken on both sides and cook over medium heat until done approx. 15 minutes. TOSS butter lettuce and spinach with dressing. SLICE each chicken breast in strips. PLACE on top of lettuce and spinach. DRIZZLE chicken with more dressing.

Dressing will keep 4 weeks refrigerated.

Yield 4 servings

la Fourchette

Pot Luck
&
Main Dishes

IV. POT LUCK AND MAIN DISHES

ARTICHOKE CHICKEN

5 lbs.	cut-up frying chicken
4 tbsp.	margarine
1- 8 oz. jar	artichoke hearts
1/2 cup	chopped onion
1/3 cup	flour
2 tsp.	dried rosemary
2 tsp.	salt
1/2 tsp.	pepper
1 cup	chicken broth
1 cup	dry white wine
1/2 lb.	whole mushrooms

In skillet BROWN chicken in margarine.
PLACE in 13" x 9" baking dish. ARRANGE
artichokes among chicken pieces. In same
skillet COOK onion until tender. BLEND in
flour, rosemary, salt and pepper. ADD
chicken broth and wine. COOK stirring until
thickened. SPOON evenly over chicken. ADD
mushrooms. BAKE 375 degrees, 50 minutes or
until bubbly.

ARTICHOKE CHICKEN can be made in
advance, covered, and refrigerated. Allow an
additional 20 minutes baking time.

Yield: 6 - 8 servings

BAKED SEAFOOD

2 lbs.	fish (shrimp, snapper, crab)
1 tbsp.	butter
1/2 cup	minced onion
1/2 lb.	mushrooms thinly sliced
1	bay leaf
1/4 cup	sherry
2-1/4 cup	medium white cream sauce
1 tbsp.	chopped chives
1/2 cup	grated cheddar cheese

In large saucepan MELT butter. ADD onions and mushrooms. SAUTE 5 minutes. ADD bay leaf, sherry and fish. COVER and COOK 3 minutes. DISCARD bay leaf. ADD cream sauce, simmer 5 minutes and ADD chives. PLACE in buttered 9"x13" BAKING PAN. TOP with cheddar cheese. BAKE 350 degrees for 30 minutes.

WHITE CREAM SAUCE:

3 tbsp.	butter
3 tbsp.	flour
1/4 tsp.	salt
2-1/2 cups	milk

In saucepan MELT butter over low heat. BLEND in flour and salt. ADD milk all at once. COOK stirring constantly until mixture thickens.

BEEF CRAB ROLLS

2 lbs.	top round steak 1/4" thick
1/4 cup	tomato juice
1	egg beaten
1 tbsp.	lemon juice
1/4 tsp.	salt
1/2 tsp.	worcestershire sauce
1 lb.	crab meat flaked
1/2 cup	fine bread crumbs
3 tbsp.	chopped parsley
2 tbsp.	oil
10 oz. can	condensed beef broth
3/4 cup	dry white wine
1 clove	garlic minced
1	bay leaf
1/2 lb.	fresh mushrooms
1 tbsp.	cornstarch
1 tbsp.	water

CUT beef into 12 rectangles. POUND to 1/8" thickness. COMBINE tomato juice, egg, lemon juice, salt, worcestershire sauce. ADD crab, bread crumbs, 1 tbsp. parsley and mix thoroughly. PLACE heaping tablespoon of filling at one end of each piece of beef. ROLL up, secure with toothpick. HEAT oil and brown rolls. PLACE in 13" x 9" baking dish. To skillet ADD broth, wine, 2 tbsp. parsley, garlic, and bay leaf and bring to boil. POUR over rolls and cover. BAKE 350 degrees 1 to 1-1/2 hours. TRANSFER to serving dish. STRAIN pan juices into two cup measure. SKIM excess fat and add water to make 1-1/2 cups. POUR into sauce pan. DISSOLVE cornstarch in water. ADD to pan juices. COOK until mixture boils. ADD mushrooms. POUR over rolls.

YIELD 6 servings.

BEEF POT PIE

2 unbaked 9" pie crusts

2 tbsp.	oil
2 lbs.	cubed chuck beef
2 med.	onions chopped
3 stalks	celery diced
2 med.	carrots diced
4 med.	potatoes peeled and diced
1 cup	turnip diced
3 tbsp.	flour
1/4 cup	water
2 tsp.	basil leaf
1/2 tsp.	garlic powder
	salt and pepper

In skillet BROWN beef in oil. DRAIN off excess oil. COVER beef with water and simmer gently until tender. ADD vegetables. COVER with water and simmer until almost tender. DISSOLVE flour in 3 tbsp. water. STIR into beef and ADD seasoning. Place 1 pie crust in a 9" pie plate and pour in beef mixture. COVER with second crust. CRIMP edges. CUT slits to allow steam to escape. BAKE 350 degrees for 30 minutes or until golden.

Yield: 4 - 6 servings

BEEF WELLINGTON

3 lbs.	eye of the round roast
1 cup	burgundy wine
1 cup	dry sherry
1	onion quartered
2	bay leaves
16 oz.	frozen puff pastry thawed
4 oz.	smooth liverwurst
1	egg lightly beaten
3/4 cup	water
3 tbsp.	flour
1/2 cup	cold water
	salt and pepper

MARINATE beef in burgundy, sherry, onion and bay leaves overnight. REMOVE from marinade, reserving sauce. ROLL out pastry 12" x 11" rectangle. SPREAD liverwurst evenly within 1/2 " edges. PLACE meat top side down in centre of pastry. DRAW up long sides to overlap. FOLD over ends. BRUSH with slightly beaten egg mixed with water. PLACE seam side down on baking sheet. BRUSH remaining egg and water mixture over all. BAKE 425 degrees 30 minutes.

SAUCE: STRAIN and heat reserved marinade. BLEND flour and cold water. ADD to marinade. Salt and pepper to taste.   COOK stirring constantly until thickened. PASS sauce when serving Beef Wellington.
Yield: 8 servings

CABBAGE ROLLS
"UNRAVELLED"

1 cup	long grain rice
3 cups	sliced cabbage
1 lb.	hamburger
2 med.	onions chopped
16 oz.	tomato sauce
1/2 tsp.	nutmeg
1 tsp.	garlic powder

COOK rice in 2 cups water until tender. PLACE in 9"x13" baking dish. COVER with sliced cabbage. In skillet BROWN hamburger and onions. DRAIN excess fat. SPREAD OVER CABBAGE. MIX together tomato sauce, nutmeg, garlic powder, salt and pepper to taste. Pour over cabbage. BAKE 350 degrees 30-45 minutes.

YIELD 6 servings.

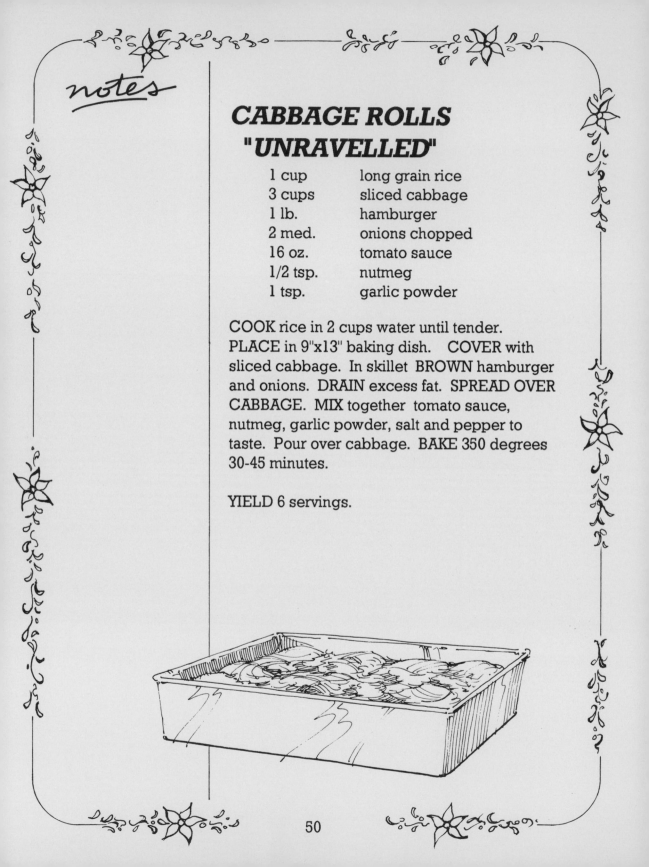

CHICKEN POT PIE

2 unbaked 9" pie crusts

2 tbsp.	margarine
1 med.	onion chopped
3 stalks	celery diced
2 med.	carrots diced
4 med.	potatoes, peeled and diced
2 med.	parsnips diced
2 cups	cooked chicken diced
3 tbsp.	flour
3 cups	chicken stock or water & 1 chicken bouillon cube
2 tsp.	tarragon
	salt and pepper

In medium size saucepan, SAUTE onion, celery, carrots, potatoes and parsnips until almost tender. ADD chicken. MIX flour into 1/2 cup water until dissolved. ADD to vegetables along with chicken broth. ADD tarragon, salt and pepper. Cook until mixture thickens. Place 1 pie crust in a 9" pie plate and pour in chicken mixture. COVER with second crust. CRIMP edges. CUT slits to allow steam to escape. BAKE 350 degrees 35-40 minutes or until golden.

Yield: 4 - 6 servings

CHICKEN CACCIATORA

1/4 cup	olive oil
3 lb.	chicken fryer cut-up
3 med.	onions diced
3 cloves	garlic chopped
16 oz. can	tomatoes
8 oz. can	tomato sauce
1 1/2 tsp.	basil
1 1/2 tsp.	oregano
2	bay leaves
1/2 cup	dry white wine
	salt and pepper to taste

In skillet BROWN chicken in olive oil.
REMOVE chicken from skillet. In same skillet
COOK onions and garlic until tender. ADD
tomatoes, tomato sauce and seasonings.
RETURN chicken to skillet. COVER. SIMMER
45 minutes. STIR in wine. Salt and pepper to
taste.   COOK uncovered another 20 minutes.

Yield: 4 serving

DON'S CHILI

2 1/2 lbs.	ground beef
2 lge.	onions chopped
4 cloves	garlic chopped
2 lge.	carrots chopped
4 stalks	celery diced
16 oz. can	kidney beans
16 oz. can	crushed tomatoes
5 1/2 oz. can	tomato paste
1 can	kernel corn
4 tbsp.	chili powder
1 tbsp.	basil
2 tsp.	dried chili peppers
3 tbsp.	vinegar
2 tbsp.	brown sugar

In large saucepan BROWN ground beef, onions and garlic. DRAIN off excess fat. ADD remaining ingredients. MIX well. Bring to a BOIL. LOWER heat and SIMMER 2 - 3 hrs. stirring often.

Yield: 8 servings

My friend Don Percy of CKLU·103 FM Winnipeg claims his chili is the best. I agree!

FISH FILLETS

1 lb.	fish fillets (any white fish)
1 cup	sour cream
2 tbsp.	minced onion
2 tbsp.	chopped green pepper
1 tbsp.	chopped parsley
1 tbsp.	lemon juice
1/2 tsp.	dry mustard
	salt and pepper to taste
	paprika

PLACE fish in baking dish. COMBINE remaining ingredients. SPREAD over fish. SPRINKLE with paprika. BAKE 375 degrees 20-30 minutes.

Yield: 4 servings

HAM WITH ORANGE AND RAISIN SAUCE

3 lb. ready to eat boneless ham
11 oz. can   Mandarin oranges
1/2 cup   brown sugar
1/2 cup   raisins*
1 tbsp.   cornstarch
1/2 tsp.   dry mustard
1/4 tsp.   ground cloves
2 tsp.   grated orange rind
1 tbsp.   lemon juice
1 tbsp.   margarine

SLICE ham into 1/2" slices. TIE slices securely back into place with string. BAKE 350 degrees 30 minutes. PLACE on serving tray. REMOVE string.

SAUCE:

DRAIN Mandarin orange juice into a 1 cup measure. ADD enough water to make 1 cup. POUR into saucepan. DISSOLVE cornstarch in juice. ADD remaining ingredients. HEAT to a boil stirring constantly. REMOVE from heat. ADD Mandarin oranges. SERVE sauce on the side.

Yield: 8 - 10 servings

*Raisins may be omitted

LASAGNA

1/2 lb.	Lasagna noodles cooked
1 cup	grated parmesan
1 cup	grated mozzarella cheese

MEAT SAUCE

1 1/2 lbs.	ground beef
1 med.	onion, chopped
3 cloves	garlic chopped
1 stalk	celery chopped
1 tbsp.	chopped parsley
1/2 med.	carrot diced
5 1/2 oz.	can tomato paste
28 oz.	can crushed tomatoes
1 tsp	basil
1 tsp.	sugar
	salt and pepper to tste

CREAM SAUCE

1/2 cup	margarine
1/2 cup	flour
4 cups	milk
1/4 tsp.	sugar
1/4 tsp.	nutmeg
1/8 tsp.	cinnamon
	salt and pepper to taste

BROWN ground beef. DRAIN excess fat. ADD meat sauce ingredients. COOK 1 hour.
CREAM SAUCE: MELT margarine. MIX in flour. ADD milk. COOK until slightly thick. ADD seasonings. OIL 13"x9" pan. LAYER noodles, meat sauce, cream sauce, parmesan, mozzarella cheese. REPEAT twice. BAKE 350 degrees 1 hour. LET sit 15 minutes before serving.   Yield: 8 servings

MACARONI AND BEEF

1/2 lb.	ground beef
1 med.	onion diced
1 cup	uncooked macaroni
16 oz.	can tomato sauce
12 oz.	can kernel corn
1 tbsp.	brown sugar
1/4 tsp.	chili powder
1/3 cup	ketchup
	salt and pepper to taste

In skillet BROWN beef. DRAIN excess fat.
PLACE in buttered 4 qt. casserole. ADD
remaining ingredients. MIX well. BAKE 325
degrees 45 minutes or until bubbly.

Yield: 6 servings

MACARONI AND CHEESE

2 cups	elbow macaroni
4 tbsp.	margarine
1 med.	onion chopped
4 tbsp.	flour
3 cups	milk
2 tbsp.	Dijon mustard
1 cup	grated cheddar cheese
1 cup	grated mozzarella cheese
	salt and pepper to taste

COOK macaroni until tender. DRAIN. MELT margarine. ADD onion. COOK until tender. MIX in flour. ADD milk gradually. COOK until thick. COMBINE macaroni, cream mixture, mustard, cheddar and mozzarella cheese. Salt and pepper to taste. PLACE in buttered 4 qt. casserole. BAKE 350 degrees 30 minutes or until bubbly.

Yield: 4 to 6 servings

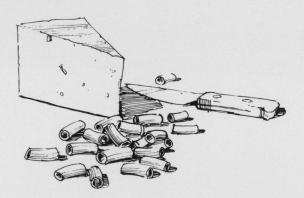

MEAT LOAF

2	eggs
2/3 cup	milk
1/2 tsp.	salt
1/2 tsp.	pepper
3 slices	fresh bread crumbled
1 med.	onion chopped
1 cup	grated carrots
2 lbs.	ground beef
1/4 cup	brown sugar
1/4 cup	ketchup
1 tbsp.	mustard

COMBINE eggs, milk, salt and pepper. ADD crumbled bread and soak until bread disintegrates. ADD onion, carrots and beef. MIX well. PACK into 9" loaf pan. BAKE 350 degrees 1 hour. POUR off excess fat. MIX sugar, ketchup and mustard. SPREAD over loaf. RETURN to oven and BAKE an additional 15 minutes. REMOVE from oven and let sit 15 minutes before removing from pan.

Yield: 6 servings

LORNIE'S SPARERIBS

2 lbs.	Baby back ribs
2 cups	Bar-B-Q sauce
1/2 cup	water
1 tsp.	worchestershire sauce
1 tsp.	soya sauce

In bowl MIX together Bar-B-Q sauce, water, worchestershire sauce and soya sauce. Place ribs in 9"x13" baking pan. COVER ribs with sauce and BAKE 400 degrees 1 hour and 20 minutes.

Yield: 4 servings

My brother Lornies' lazy gourmet ribs This is it ?

SALMON LOAF

1 cup	macaroni cooked
2 tbsp.	margarine
1 med.	onion diced
1 med.	carrot diced
1/2 cup	diced celery
1 cup	cooked salmon, flaked
1 1/2 cups	milk
2	eggs beaten
1 tsp.	dill weed
	salt and pepper to taste
1/4 cup	grated parmesan cheese
	paprika

In skillet MELT margarine. ADD onion, carrots and celery. COOK until tender. ADD to macaroni along with salmon, milk, eggs and dill weed. MIX well. Salt and pepper to taste. PACK into buttered 9" loaf pan. TOP with parmesan cheese. SPRINKLE with paprika. BAKE 325 degrees 35-40 minutes or until bubbly.

SALMON BAKED IN MAYONNAISE

5 lb.	salmon, skinned and boned
1 lge.	onion sliced
3 stalks	celery cut in 1" pieces
1 tsp.	salt
1 tsp.	pepper
1/2 tsp.	basil
1/2 tsp.	dill weed
1 1/2 cups	mayonnaise

STUFF salmon with onion, celery and seasonings. PLACE on oiled foil-lined baking sheet. TIE salmon at ends with string to hold together. SPREAD mayonnaise on top and sides of salmon.
BAKE 45- 50 minutes.

Yield: 6-8 servings

SHEPHERD'S PIE

2 tbsp.	margarine
1 lge.	onion chopped
2 lge.	carrots peeled and chopped
2 stalks	celery diced
1/2 lb.	mushrooms sliced
2 lbs.	lean ground beef
3 tbsp.	flour
3 tbsp.	water
1 cup	beef broth
2 tsp.	worchestershire sauce
2 tbsp.	ketchup
1 tsp.	basil
	salt and pepper to taste
2 lbs.	potatoes peeled & cooked
2 tbsp.	margarine
1/4 cup	milk

In large saucepan MELT margarine. ADD onions, celery, carrots and mushrooms. SAUTE until tender. ADD beef. COOK until browned. DRAIN excess fat. DISSOLVE flour in water. STIR into meat mixture. ADD broth, worcestershire sauce, ketchup, basil, salt and pepper to taste. HEAT thoroughly. PLACE in 9"x13" baking pan. MASH potatoes. BEAT in margarine and milk until fluffy. SPREAD over meat mixture. DOT with margarine. BAKE 350 degrees 45 minutes or until topping is browned.

Yield: 6 servings

SMOKED SALMON CREPES

1 1/2 lbs.	smoked salmon
24	crepes

SAUCE
2 tbsp.	margarine
2 tbsp.	flour
1 cup	milk
1	egg yolk beaten
2 ozs.	grated cheddar cheese
4 oz.	can baby shrimp, drained

PLACE 1 oz. smoked salmon in centre of each crepe and roll up. PLACE in buttered shallow baking dish. MELT margarine. BLEND in flour. STIR in milk. COOK over low heat until mixture begins to thicken. STIR a little sauce into egg yolk. ADD to the sauce along with cheese. STIR until sauce begins to bubble and cheese has melted. ADD shrimp. POUR over crepes. BAKE 375 degrees 10-15 minutes.

Yield: 6-8 servings

STEAK SANDWICH MUSHROOM SAUCE

4 - 6	tenderloin steaks
4 - 6 slices	French bread, 2" thick

MUSHROOM SAUCE

6 tbsp.	margarine
1 lb.	fresh mushrooms sliced
1 medium	onion, minced
2 tbsp.	flour
2 tsp.	soya sauce
1 1/2 cups	milk

BROIL or BAR-B-Q steaks to personal preference. TOAST bread. MELT margarine. ADD mushrooms and onions. COOK until tender. MIX in flour. ADD soya sauce. STIR in milk slowly. COOK and STIR until sauce thickens. DIP French bread in sauce. PLACE steak on top. DRIZZLE with additional sauce.

Yield: 4 - 6 servings

STIFADO

2 lbs	cubed chuck beef
1/4 cup	oil
4 lge.	onions sliced
5 1/2 oz.	can tomato paste
1/3 cup	water
2 tbsp.	vinegar
2 tbsp.	brown sugar
1 clove	garlic chopped
1	bay leaf
1/4 tsp.	cinnamon
1/2 tsp.	ground cloves
1/2 tsp.	cumin
2 tbsp.	raisins

In skillet BROWN beef in oil. TRANSFER beef to 3 qt. baking dish. MIX remaining ingredients together. ADD to beef. BAKE covered 325 degrees 1 3/4 hrs.

Yield: 6 servings

TURKEY TETTRAZZINI

16 ozs.	spaghetti cooked
1/4 cup	margarine
1 1/2 cups	diced celery
1 cup	diced green pepper
1 lge.	onion, diced
1/2 lb.	mushrooms, thinly sliced
1/4 cup	flour
2 cups	milk
1/2 lb.	cheddar cheese grated
2 tsp.	salt
1/4 tsp.	pepper
1/2 tsp.	marjoram
2 cups	cooked turkey meat diced
1/4 cup	sherry
1/4 cup	parmesan cheese

MELT margarine. ADD celery, green pepper, onion and mushrooms. SAUTE until tender. BLEND in flour. ADD milk and cook until creamy. ADD grated cheese, salt, pepper, marjoram, turkey and sherry. MIX spaghetti and sauce together. POUR into buttered 4 qt. baking dish. SPRINKLE with parmesan cheese. BAKE 350 degrees 25-30 minutes.

Yield: 6 servings

notes

notes

VEGETABLE STUFFED BURGERS

2 tbsp.	margarine
2 medium	potatoes grated
1 medium	carrot grated
1 medium	zucchini grated
1/2 medium	onion grated
1 cup	finely chopped mushrooms
3 tbsp.	bread crumbs
1 tsp.	oregano
	salt and pepper to taste
2 lbs.	lean ground beef
1 cup	bread crumbs
2	eggs beaten
1/4 cup	chopped parsley
2 tsp.	garlic powder

In medium saucepan MELT margarine. ADD vegetables. COOK until tender. ADD bread crumbs and seasoning. MIX well. In bowl MIX ground beef, bread crumbs, eggs, parsley and garlic powder. FORM patties about 4" in diameter. SPREAD 2 tbsp. stuffing on one patty. TOP with another patty. SEAL edges. PLACE on baking sheet. BAKE 350 degrees 30 minutes.

TOPPING: 1/4 cup ketchup
                2 tbsp. Dijon mustard
                2 tbsp. brown sugar

MIX thoroughly together. SPOON on top of baked burgers. RETURN to oven and bake 5 minutes more. SERVE on jumbo Kaisers Buns.

Yield: 6 burgers

la Fourchette

Vegetables
&
Rice

V. VEGETABLES & RICE

BAKED GARLIC

6	whole heads of garlic
4 tbsp.	margarine
1/2 cup	chicken broth

REMOVE papery outer skin from garlic leaving the cluster intact. PLACE in small baking dish. ADD margarine and chicken broth. BAKE 350 degrees 1 hour, basting every 15 minutes.

Yield 6 servings

GINGER CARROTS

6 med.	carrots peeled cooked and cut diagonally in 1" pieces
1 tbsp.	margarine
1 tbsp.	brown sugar
2 tbsp.	minced fresh ginger
4 tbsp.	water

PLACE carrots in buttered 2 qt. baking dish.
ADD margarine, sugar, ginger and water.
COVER. BAKE 350 degrees 20 minutes.

Yield 4-6 servings

HERB RICE

1 cup	chopped onion
1 cup	uncooked rice
3 tbsp.	margarine
3 cubes	chicken bouillion
1/2 tsp.	margoram
1/2 tsp.	savory
1/2 tsp.	rosemary
1/2 tsp.	salt
2 cups	hot water

In medium saucepan BROWN onions and rice in margarine. ADD herbs and salt. DISSOLVE chicken bouillon cubes in hot water. MIX into rice. COVER and cook until dry.

Yield: 4 servings

MARINATED MUSHROOMS

1 lb.	small mushrooms
1-3/4 cup	water
1/2 cup	olive oil
	juice of 1 lemon
2 tbsp.	vinegar
1 tsp.	salt
1 stalk	celery with leaves quartered
4 sprigs	parsley
8	peppercorns
6	coriander seeds
1/2 tsp.	thyme
1/4 tsp.	fennel seeds
1 tbsp.	chopped fresh parsley

WIPE mushrooms. In medium saucepan COMBINE water, oil, lemon juice, vinegar, and salt. TIE celery, parsley, peppercorns, coriander seeds, thyme, and fennel seeds in cheesecloth. ADD to the liquid. BRING to boil. REDUCE heat and simmer covered 5 minutes. ADD mushrooms. COVER and refrigerate. When ready to serve DRAIN and sprinkle with parsley.

Yield 4 servings

ONION PUDDING

1 lb.	onion thinly sliced
2 tbsp.	margarine
2	eggs
1 tsp. each	salt and pepper
2/3 cup	milk
1/4 cup	flour

In medium saucepan STEW onions in margarine over low heat for 1/2 hour. WHISK together eggs, salt, pepper, milk and flour until smooth. STIR into the onions. POUR into liberally buttered 2 qt. baking dish. BAKE 450 degrees 20-25 minutes or until well browned.

Yield 4-6 servings

SCALLOPED POTATOES

8	raw potatoes peeled and sliced
1 med.	onion diced
6 tbsp.	flour
1 tsp. each	salt and pepper
2 tsp.	garlic powder
6 cups	milk
2 tbsp.	butter

In small bowl MIX flour, salt, pepper and garlic powder together. In liberally buttered 4 qt. baking dish PLACE one layer of potatoes, half of the onions and half of the flour mixture. REPEAT ending with a top layer of potatoes. POUR milk over all. DOT with butter. BAKE 350 degrees 1 to 1-1/2 hours or until tender.

Yield 6-8 servings

SPICY GREEN BEANS

4 tsp.	chili oil
1/2 tsp.	salt
4 lge.	garlic cloves minced
2 tbsp.	fresh minced ginger
4 cups	oil
2 lbs.	fresh green beans

MIX chili oil, salt, garlic and ginger together in small bowl. SET aside. HEAT wok on high heat. ADD oil and HEAT to 380 degrees. DEEP fry beans for 1-2 minutes. They should be wrinkled and blistered but still bright green. DRAIN beans, leaving 1 tbsp. oil in wok. RETURN wok to high heat. ADD chili oil mixture. COOK for several seconds. RETURN beans to wok. STIR-FRY until beans are coated, approx. 1 minute. SERVE hot.

Yield 6 servings

THE COMMODORE'S BARLEY PILAF

4	dry mushrooms
1 cup	hot water
5 tbsp.	margarine
2 med.	onions chopped
1/2 lb.	fresh mushrooms thinly sliced
1-3/4 cup	pot barley
	salt and pepper to taste
4 cups	consomme

SOAK dry mushrooms in hot water for 1 hour. RESERVE water. CUT mushrooms in slivers. SET aside. MELT 3 tbsp. margarine in frying pan. ADD onions and fresh mushrooms. TOSS over medium heat 5 minutes. REMOVE from pan and set aside. In same pan melt 2 tbsp. margarine. ADD barley. STIR until barley is browned. PLACE barley in buttered baking dish. ADD mushroom slivers, onions, fresh mushrooms, salt and pepper. POUR reserved mushroom water and 4 cups consomme over all. COVER. BAKE 350 degrees 1 hour.

YIELD 6-8 servings

My sister, Laraine, gave me this recipe a long time ago. I use it frequently when catering.

la Fourchette

Muffins

VI.   MUFFINS

APPLE CINNAMON MUFFINS

3 cups	flour
1 cup	brown sugar
2 1/4 tsp.	baking powder
3/4 tsp.	baking soda
1-1/2 tsp.	salt
1 tbsp.	cinnamon
2 cups	peeled, diced apples
2	eggs
1 cup	oil
1 cup	buttermilk

MIX dry ingredients together. ADD apples.
WHISK eggs and oil together until slightly
thick. ADD to dry ingredients along with
buttermilk. FOLD together until all dry ingredients are blended. FILL well oiled muffin
pan to the top. BAKE 350 degrees 30 minutes
or until muffins are dry on top.

Yield: 1 dozen

BANANA RAISIN BRAN MUFFINS

2 cups	wholewheat flour
2 cups	bran
1 cup	brown sugar
1 1/4 cups	wheatgerm
2 1/4 tsp.	baking soda
1 1/4 tsp.	salt
2 cups	chopped bananas*
1 cup	golden raisins**
2	eggs
1 cup	vegetable oil
1 cup	buttermilk

MIX dry ingredients together. MIX in bananas and raisins. WHISK eggs and oil until slightly thick. ADD to dry ingredients along with buttermilk. FOLD together until all dry ingredients are blended. FILL well oiled muffin pan to the top. BAKE 350 degrees 30 minutes or until tops are dry.   Yield: 1 dozen

*FOR VARIATION omit bananas and add 2 cups of any of the following:

    Blueberries, fresh or frozen
    Pineapple Tidbits
    Chopped peaches
    Grated zucchini

**Raisins may be omitted

CARROT PINEAPPLE MUFFINS

2 1/4 cups	flour
1 1/2 cups	brown sugar
1 1/2 tsp.	baking powder
1 1/2 tsp.	baking soda
1 tsp.	salt
1 1/2 tsp.	cinnamon
1 1/2 cups	grated carrots
3/4 cup	pineapple tidbits
2	eggs
1 cup	oil
1 1/2 tsp.	vanilla
1 cup	buttermilk

MIX dry ingredients together. ADD carrots and pineapple tidbits. WHISK eggs, oil and vanilla together until slightly thick. ADD to dry ingredients along with buttermilk. FOLD together until all dry ingredients are blended. FILL well oiled muffin pan to the top. BAKE 350 degrees 30 minutes or until tops are dry.

Yield: 1 dozen

CHEESE PINEAPPLE MUFFINS

3 cups	flour
1 1/2 cups	sugar
1 1/2 tsp.	baking powder
3/4 tsp.	baking soda
1 1/2 tsp.	salt
1 cup	pineapple tidbits
1 cup	grated cheddar cheese
2	eggs
1 cup	vegetable oil
1 tsp.	vanilla
1 cup	buttermilk

MIX dry ingredients together. ADD pineapple tidbits and cheddar cheese. WHISK together eggs, oil and vanilla until slightly thick. ADD to dry ingredients along with buttermilk. FOLD together until all dry ingredients are blended. FILL well oiled muffin pan to the top. BAKE 350 degrees 30 minutes or until tops are dry.

Yield: 1 dozen

BLUEBERRY ORANGE MUFFINS

3 cups	flour
1 1/4 cups	sugar
2 1/4 tsp.	baking powder
3/4 tsp.	baking soda
1 1/2 tsp.	salt
2 cups	blueberries
1 tbsp.	grated orange rind
2	eggs
1 cup	vegetable oil
3/4 cup	orange juice

MIX dry ingredients together. ADD blueberries and orange rind. WHISK eggs and oil together until slightly thick. ADD to dry ingredients along with orange juice. FOLD together until all dry ingredients are blended. FILL well oiled muffin pan to the top. BAKE 350 degrees 30 minutes or until tops are dry.

Yield: 1 dozen

DATE OATMEAL MUFFINS

2 1/2 cups	flour
2 1/2 cups	large oats
1 1/4 cups	brown sugar
2 1/4 tsp.	baking powder
1 tsp.	baking soda
1 1/4 tsp.	salt
2 cups	chopped dates*
2	eggs
1 cup	vegetable oil
1 cup	buttermilk

MIX dry ingredients together. ADD dates. WHISK eggs and oil together until slightly thick. ADD to dry ingredients along with buttermilk. FOLD together until all dry ingredients are blended. FILL well oiled muffin pan to the top. BAKE 350 degrees 30 minutes or until tops are dry.

Yield: 1 dozen

*FOR VARIATION omit dates and add 2 cups blueberries or cranberries.

HAM AND CHEESE MUFFINS

3 cups	flour
1 cup	sugar
1 1/4 tsp.	baking soda
1 tsp.	salt
2 tsp.	oregano
1 cup	grated cheddar cheese
1/2 cup	diced ham
1/2 cup	chopped green onion
2	eggs
1 cup	vegetable oil
1 cup	buttermilk

MIX dry ingredients together. ADD cheese, ham and green onions. WHISK together eggs and oil until slightly thick. ADD to dry ingredients along with buttermilk. FOLD until all dry ingredients are blended. FILL well oiled muffin pan to the top. BAKE 350 degrees 30 minutes or until tops are dry.

MANDARIN ORANGE MUFFINS

~~1 1/2 cups~~	flour
1/2 cup	sugar
2 1/2 tsp.	baking powder
1/4 tsp.	salt
1/4 tsp.	ground allspice
1/2 tsp.	nutmeg
2	eggs
1 cup	oil
1 cup	buttermilk
6 oz. can	mandarin oranges

MIX dry ingredients together. WHISK eggs and oil together until slightly thick. ADD to dry ingredients along with buttermilk and mandarin oranges (including juice). FOLD until all dry ingredients are blended. FILL well oiled muffin pan. BAKE 350 degrees 30 minutes or until tops are dry.

Yield: ~~6~~ large muffins

POPPYSEED MUFFINS

3 cups	flour
1 cup	sugar
1 1/4 tsp.	baking soda
1 tsp.	salt
2 tsp.	grated orange rind
1/4 cup	whole poppyseeds
2	eggs
1 cup	vegetable oil
1 cup	buttermilk
11/2 tsp.	vanilla

MIX dry ingredients together. WHISK eggs and oil together until slightly thick. ADD to dry ingredients along with buttermilk and vanilla. Fold together until all dry ingredients are blended. FILL well oiled muffin pan to the top. BAKE 350 degrees 30 minutes or until tops are dry.

Yield: 1 dozen

PUMPKIN MUFFINS

4 1/2 cups	wholewheat flour
2 cup	brown sugar
3 3/4 tsp.	baking powder
1 1/2 tsp.	baking soda
1/2 tsp.	cinnamon
1/2 tsp.	ground cloves
1 tsp.	nutmeg
1/2 tsp.	ground ginger
1 1/2 tsp.	salt
1 1/2 cups	pumpkin
3	eggs
1 1/2 cups	oil
1/2 cup	buttermilk

MIX dry ingredients together. WHISK eggs and oil together until slightly thick. ADD to dry ingredients along with buttermilk and pumpkin. FOLD together until all dry ingredients are blended. FILL well oiled muffin pan to the top. BAKE 350 degrees or until tops are dry.

Yield: 1 dozen

la Fourchette

Tea Breads
&
Cookies

VII. TEA BREADS AND COOKIES

BANANA BREAD

3/4 cup	margarine
2 cups	sugar
8	eggs
2 tsp.	vanilla
2 cups	mashed bananas
4 cups	flour
2 tsp.	baking soda
2 tsp.	baking powder
1 cup	buttermilk

CREAM margarine and sugar. BEAT in eggs one at a time. ADD vanilla and bananas. SIFT together flour, baking soda and baking powder. BEAT into cream mixture alternately with buttermilk. POUR into 2 oiled 9" loaf pans. BAKE 350 degrees 45-50 minutes or until toothpick inserted comes out clean.

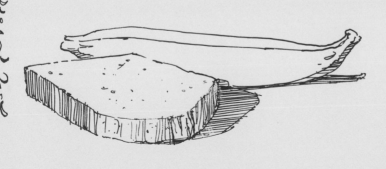

BLUEBERRY NUT LOAF

2/3 cup	margarine
1 1/3 cup	sugar
4	eggs
2 cups	mashed bananas
3 cups	flour
4 1/2 tsp.	baking powder
1 tsp.	salt
1 cup	oatmeal
1 cup	blueberries
1 cup	walnuts chopped

CREAM margarine and sugar. ADD eggs and bananas and MIX well. COMBINE flour, baking powder, salt and oatmeal. MIX into creamed mixture. STIR in blueberries and walnuts. POUR into 2 oiled 9" loaf pans. BAKE 350 degrees 1 hour or until toothpick inserted comes out clean.

This Bread freezes beautifully.

Yield: 2 loaves

My sister and I skip home with a full pail of blueberries for our Moms' baking

CHOCOLATE ZUCCHINI ORANGE BREAD

2 cups	sugar
1/2 cup	oil
3	eggs
1 tsp.	vanilla
2 cups	flour
1/2 cup	cocoa
1 tsp.	baking powder
1 tsp.	baking soda
1/2 tsp.	nutmeg
1/2 tsp.	salt
2/3 cup	buttermilk
2 cups	grated zucchini
1 tbsp.	grated orange rind

CREAM sugar and oil together. BEAT in vanilla and eggs one at a time. MIX the flour, cocoa, baking powder, baking soda, nutmeg and salt together. BEAT into creamed mixture alternately with the buttermilk. ADD orange rind and grated zucchini. POUR batter into 2 oiled 9" loaf pans. BAKE 350 degrees or until toothpick inserted comes out clean. REMOVE from pans and cool.

TOPPING:
1/2 cup icing sugar
2 1/2 tsp. orange juice
1 tsp. grated orange rind
1/2 tsp. margarine

COMBINE in saucepan all topping ingredients. BRING to a boil stirring constantly. BRUSH over top of cooled loaves.

LEMON BREAD

1 cup	margarine
2 cups	sugar
4	eggs
3 cups	flour
2 tsp.	baking powder
1 tsp.	salt
2 tbsp.	grated lemon rind
1 cup	milk

CREAM margarine and sugar. BEAT in eggs one at a time. SIFT together flour, baking powder, salt and lemon rind. BEAT gradually into the creamed mixture alternately with the milk. POUR into oiled 9" loaf pan. BAKE 350 degrees about 40 minutes or until toothpick inserted comes out clean. REMOVE from pan and cool.

TOPPING:
2/3 cup sugar
1/2 cup lemon juice

In saucepan combine sugar and lemon juice. Bring to a BOIL stirring constantly. REMOVE from heat and BRUSH over loaf.

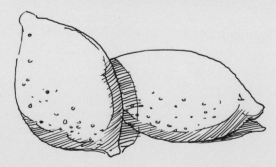

BIRDS-IN-THE-NEST

1/2 cup	margarine
1/4 cup	sugar
1	egg separated
2 tsp.	lemon juice
1 cup	flour
1 cup	walnuts chopped fine

CREAM together margarine and sugar. ADD egg yolk, lemon juice, flour and beat well. SHAPE dough into 1" balls. DIP into egg white and roll in walnuts. MAKE dent in center of each cookie with a thimble. BAKE 325 degrees for 5 minutes. MAKE dent again. BAKE for another 10 - 15 minutes or until golden. COOL and FILL cookie center with stawberry jam.

Yield: 2 1/2 dozen

DAD'S RAISIN COOKIES

1 cup	margarine
1 cup	sugar
1/2 cup	brown sugar
1	egg
1 1/2 cups	flour
1 1/2 cups	rolled oats
1 cup	coconut
1 tsp.	baking soda
1 tsp.	baking powder
1 tbsp.	molasses
1/2 tsp.	cinnamon
1 tsp.	allspice
1 tsp.	nutmeg
1 cup	raisins

CREAM margarine and sugar. ADD egg. MIX dry ingredients together and gradually beat into creamed mixture. STIR in raisins. BAKE 325 degrees 20 - 25 minutes.

Yield: 2 1/2 dozen

MOM'S CHOCOLATE CHIP COOKIES

1 1/2 cups	margarine
1 1/3 cups	sugar
1 cup	brown sugar packed
4	eggs
1 tbsp.	vanilla
1 tsp.	lemon juice
3 cups	flour
2 tsp.	baking soda
1 1/2 tsp.	salt
1 tsp.	cinnamon
1 1/2 cups	oatmeal
4 cups	chocolate chips
2 cups	walnuts chopped

CREAM margarine and sugars. BEAT in eggs one at a time with vanilla and lemon juice. SIFT flour, baking soda, salt and cinnamon together and BEAT into creamed mixture gradually. MIX in oatmeal. FOLD in chocolate chips and walnuts. DROP by heaping tablespoon onto greased cookie sheet 1" apart. BAKE 350 degrees 12 - 15 minutes.

Yield: 4 dozen

notes

PEANUT BUTTER COOKIES

1 cup	margarine
1 cup	sugar
1 cup	brown sugar
2	eggs
1 tsp.	vanilla
1 cup	peanut butter
2 1/4 cups	flour
2 tsp.	baking soda
1/2 tsp.	salt

CREAM margarine and sugars together. BEAT in eggs one at a time along with vanilla. STIR in peanut butter. BEAT in flour, baking soda and salt. LIGHTLY flour your hands. ROLL a heaping tablespoon of batter into a ball. PLACE on ungreased cookie sheet 1" apart. LIGHTLY flatten with fork dipped in flour. BAKE 325 degrees 10 - 15 minutes or until golden.

Yield: 3 dozen

SHORTBREAD COOKIES

1 lb.	butter
1 1/2 cups	icing sugar
1/2 cup	cornstarch
1/2 tsp.	almond extract
3 cups	flour

CREAM butter, icing sugar and cornstarch. ADD almond extract. GRADUALLY BEAT in flour. KNEAD on lightly floured surface for 3 minutes. ROLL out 1/4" thick. CUT out with cookie cutters. BAKE 325 degrees 15 - 20 minutes or until golden. COOL. DECORATE with a dab of icing and 1/4 of a maraschino cherry.

Yield: 2 dozen

THE MONSTER COOKIE

1 lb.	margarine
2 cups	white sugar
1 cup	brown sugar
2	eggs
2 cups	flour
2 tsp.	baking powder
2 tsp.	baking soda
2 cups	old fashion oats
2 cups	coconut
1 cup	chocolate chips

CREAM together margarine and sugars. BEAT in eggs one at a time. MIX together flour, baking powder and baking soda. BEAT into creamed mixture. MIX in by hand, the oats, coconut and chocolate chips. Lightly flour your hands and shape cookie dough into balls the size of golf balls. PLACE on oiled cookie sheet 2" apart. BAKE 325 degrees 20 - 25 minutes or until browned.

Yield: Yield: 4 dozen

This cookie dough freezes very well. Shape the cookie dough before freezing. Let the frozen cookie dough thaw before baking.

la Fourchette

Cakes
Squares
&
Desserts

VIII. SQUARES, CAKES AND DESSERTS

CANDY BARS

1/2 cup	margarine
1/4 cup	brown sugar
2 cups	quick cooking oats
1/4 cup	liquid honey
1/2 cup	peanut butter
1/2 cup	chocolate chips
1/4 cup	unsalted peanuts

CREAM margarine and sugar together. STIR in oats and honey. PRESS into buttered 8" square pan. BAKE 350 degrees 20 minutes. COOL COMPLETELY.

In saucepan over medium heat MELT peanut butter and chocolate chips.

SPREAD over cooked base and sprinkle with peanuts.

CHILL until firm. Cut into squares.

CHEESECAKE BROWNIES

1/2 cup	margarine
1-1/2 cup	white sugar
2	eggs
1/2 cup	cocoa
1-1/2 tsp.	vanilla
1 cup	cream cheese
1	egg
2/3 cup	flour
1/2 tsp.	baking powder
1/4 tsp.	salt

CREAM margarine and 1 cup sugar. BEAT in eggs, cocoa and 1 tsp. vanilla. POUR 1/2 of the batter into oiled 9" square pan. RESERVE other 1/2 of batter. BEAT together cream cheese, 1/2 cup sugar, egg and 1/2 tsp. vanilla. MIX in flour, baking powder and salt. SPREAD evenly over batter in pan. COVER with reserved batter. PULL knife through in three straight lines.

BAKE 350 degrees 40 minutes.

Cut into squares.

LA FOURCHETTE CAKE-TYPE BROWNIES

1/2 cup	margarine
2	eggs
1 tsp.	vanilla
1-2/3 cup	flour
1-1/2 cup	sugar
2/3 cup	cocoa
1-1/2 tsp.	baking soda
1 tsp.	salt
1-1/2 cup	buttermilk
1 cup	chopped walnuts

CREAM margarine and eggs. ADD vanilla.
MIX together flour, sugar, cocoa, baking soda
and salt. Gradually beat dry ingredients into
creamed mixture alternately with buttermilk.
ADD nuts. POUR into oiled 9"x13" pan. BAKE
350 degrees 35-40 minutes.

ICING:

3 tbsp.	margarine
1/4 cup	cream cheese
2 cups	icing sugar
3 tbsp.	cocoa

BEAT margarine, cream cheese, icing sugar
and cocoa together until creamy. SPREAD
over cooled brownies.

MAPLE WALNUT SQUARES

1/2 cup	margarine
1/2 cup	brown sugar
1 cup	flour

MIX together until crumbly. PRESS firmly into buttered 8" square buttered pan. BAKE 350 degrees 10 minutes.

2	eggs beaten
1 cup	brown sugar
1/2 cup	chopped walnuts
2 tbsp.	flour
1/2 tsp.	baking powder
1/2 tsp.	vanilla

BEAT all ingredients together. POUR over base evenly. RETURN to oven and BAKE an additional 20 - 25 minutes.

ICING

3 tbsp.	margarine
1/4 cup	cream cheese
2 cups	icing sugar

BEAT all ingredients together until creamy. SPREAD over cooled squares.

MARSHMALLOW GRAHAM SQUARES

1/2 cup	butter or margarine
2	eggs
1 cup	sugar
1/4 cup	coconut
1 tsp.	vanilla
2-1/4 cup	fine graham crumbs
1/2 cup	chopped walnuts
3 cups	miniature marshmallows

MELT butter in top of double boiler. ADD eggs, sugar, coconut and vanilla. COOK over simmering water 10 minutes or until thick. REMOVE from heat. MIX in graham crumbs, walnuts and marshmallows. PACK into buttered 8" square pan. CHILL.

BUTTER ICING:

2 tbsp.	soft butter or margarine
1-1/2 cup	sifted icing sugar
1-1/2 tsp.	milk
3/4 tsp.	vanilla

BEAT all ingredients until fluffy.

NANAIMO BARS

1/2 lb.	margarine
1/2 cup	liquid honey
1/2 cup	sugar
1/2 cup	cocoa
2 cups	coconut
2 cups	toasted almond slices
1-1/2 cup	graham crumbs

MELT margarine and honey over low heat. ADD remaining ingredients. PRESS firmly into 9"x13" buttered pan. CHILL.

FILLING:

1/2 lb.	margarine
1/2 cup	Birds Eye Custard
1-1/2 cups	icing sugar
1 tbsp.	milk

BEAT margarine until creamy. Gradually ADD custard, icing sugar and milk. BEAT 3-4 minutes. SPREAD evenly over base. CHILL.

TOPPING:

8 oz.	semi-sweet chocolate
1 tbsp.	margarine
1 tbsp.	whipping cream

MELT chocolate and margarine. STIR in cream. SPREAD evenly over filling. REFRIGERATE until set.

PUMPKIN SQUARES

1	yellow cake mix
1/2 cup	melted margarine
4	eggs
16 oz.	canned or fresh pumpkin
2/3 cup	milk
1/2 cup	brown sugar
2 tsp.	cinnamon
1/2 tsp.	nutmeg
1/2 tsp.	ground cloves
1 tsp.	vanilla
1/2 cup	white sugar
1/4 cup	cold margarine
1/2 cup	chopped nuts
2 oz.	melted semi-sweet chocolate

RESERVE 1 cup of cake mix. MIX remaining cake mix with melted margarine and 1 egg. PRESS into 9"x13" oiled pan. MIX pumpkin, 3 eggs, milk, brown sugar, spices and vanilla together. POUR over cake dough. MIX reserved cake mix with white sugar and margarine until crumbly. SPRINKLE over pumpkin mixture then SPRINKLE with nuts. BAKE 350 degrees 45-50 minutes. DRIZZLE with melted chocolate.

notes

notes

QUALICUM BARS

1/2 cup	brown sugar
1/2 cup	light corn syrup
1 cup	smooth peanut butter
1 cup	rice krispies
1 cup	corn flakes

FILLING

2 cups	icing sugar
3 tbsp.	Birds Eye Custard
1/4 cup	margarine
3 tbsp.	milk

TOPPING

4 oz.	semi-sweet chocolate
2 tbsp.	margarine
2 tbsp.	milk

COOK over low heat brown sugar, corn syrup and peanut butter until melted. MIX in Rice Krispies and corn flakes. PAT into 9" square pan. CHILL. BEAT icing sugar, custard powder, margarine and milk until fluffy. SPREAD evenly over base. MELT chocolate and margarine. ADD milk and cook until well blended. SPREAD evenly over filling. CHILL.

APPLE WALNUT COCONUT CAKE

2 cups	white sugar
3	eggs
1-1/4 cup	oil
1/4 tsp.	salt
1/4 cup	orange juice
3 cups	white flour
1 tsp.	baking soda
1 tsp.	cinnamon
1 tsp.	vanilla
1 cup	peeled cored finely chopped apples
1 cup	coconut
1 cup	chopped walnuts

BEAT together sugar, eggs, oil, salt and orange juice. SIFT together the flour, baking soda, and cinnamon. Gradually beat into first mixture along with vanilla. STIR in apples, coconut and walnuts. POUR into oiled Bundt cake pan. BAKE 350 degrees 40-45 minutes or until cake springs back when lightly touched. REMOVE from pan. COOL.

TOPPING:

6 tbsp.	butter
1 cup	sugar
1/2 tsp.	baking soda
1/2 cup	buttermilk

MELT butter in saucepan. ADD sugar, baking soda and buttermilk. COOK until bubbly. SPOON over cake.

BANANA CHOCOLATE CAKE

1/4 cup	margarine
1 cup	sugar
4	eggs
1 tsp.	vanilla
1 cup	mashed bananas
2 cups	flour
1 tsp.	baking soda
1 tsp.	baking powder
1/2 cup	buttermilk

CREAM margarine and sugar. While beating, ADD eggs one at a time. Along with vanilla and bananas. MIX flour, baking soda and baking powder together. BEAT into cream mixture a little at a time. MIX in buttermilk. POUR into 9"x13" oiled pan. BAKE 350 degrees 40-45 minutes or until center springs back. REMOVE from pan. COOL. SLICE cake lengthwise in half. SPREAD 1/2 of the chocolate icing on one piece. COVER with sliced bananas. TOP with other half. SPREAD rest of icing on top and sides of cake. PLACE sliced bananas on top to finish cake.

CHOCOLATE ICING:

1/2 cup	margarine
1 cup	cream cheese
2 cup	icing sugar
6 tbsp.	cocoa
6 tbsp.	milk

BEAT margarine and cream cheese until creamy. ADD icing sugar, cocoa and milk. BEAT until fluffy.

CHOCOLATE FUDGE BUNDT CAKE

4 cups	flour
3 cups	sugar
6 tbsp.	cocoa
1 tbsp.	baking soda
3 cups	hot coffee
1 cup	oil
2 tbsp.	white vinegar
1 tbsp.	vanilla

MIX together flour, sugar, cocoa and baking soda. WHISK together coffee, oil, vinegar, and vanilla until well blended. ADD to flour mixture and BEAT well. POUR into oiled Bundt cake pan. BAKE 350 degrees 40 minutes or until cake springs back when lightly touched. REMOVE from pan and cool.

TOPPING:

1 cup	cream cheese
1 cup	icing sugar
1 tbsp.	cocoa
1 tbsp.	coffee
1 tbsp.	milk

BEAT cream cheese, icing sugar, cocoa, coffee, and milk until fluffy. TOP each slice of cake with a dollop of this topping.

LA FOURCHETTE CARROT CAKE

2 cups	brown sugar
2 cups	oil
6	eggs
2 cups	white flour
2-1/2 tsp.	salt
2-1/2 tsp.	baking soda
2-1/2 tsp.	baking powder
4 cups	grated carrots
1 cup	chopped nuts

BEAT together brown sugar, oil and eggs. MIX dry ingredients together. ADD to liquid ingredients while BEATING slowly. STIR in carrots and nuts. BAKE 350 degrees approx. 45 minutes or until top springs back.

ICING:

1/2 cup	margarine
1/2 cup	cream cheese
2 1/2 cups	icing sugar
1 tsp.	vanilla

BEAT all ingredients together until creamy. SPREAD over cooled cake.

MOM'S CARROT PINEAPPLE CAKE

2 cups	oil
2 cups	white sugar
3	eggs
3-1/2 cups	flour
1-1/4 tsp.	baking soda
1-1/4 tsp.	baking powder
2-1/2 cups	grated carrots
14 oz. can	crushed pineapple
2 cups	chopped walnuts
1 cup	shredded coconut

BEAT oil, sugar, and eggs. ADD remaining ingredients. POUR into greased 9"x13" pan. BAKE 350 degrees approx. 1 hour or until centre springs back. REMOVE from pan. COOL.

ICING:

1/2 cup	margarine
1/2 cup	cream cheese
2-1/2 cups	icing sugar
1 tsp.	vanilla

BEAT until creamy.

POPPYSEED CAKE

1 cup	margarine
1-1/2 cup	white sugar
4	eggs
2 cups	flour
1 tsp.	baking soda
1 tsp.	vanilla
1/2 cup	whole poppyseeds
1 cup	sour cream

CREAM margarine and sugar. BEAT in eggs one at a time. MIX in flour and baking soda. STIR in poppyseeds and sour cream until well blended. POUR into oiled 9"x 13" pan. BAKE 325 degrees 40-45 minutes or until center springs back when lightly touched.

ICING:

1/2 cup	margarine
2-1/2 cups	icing sugar
1/2 cup	cream cheese
1 tsp.	vanilla

BEAT margarine, icing sugar, cream cheese and vanilla together until fluffy.

STRAWBERRY SOUR CREAM CAKE

1/2 cup	margarine
1 cup	sugar
3	eggs
2 cups	flour
1 tsp.	baking soda
1/2 tsp.	salt
1 tsp.	vanilla
1 cup	sour cream
2 cups	fresh sliced strawberries*

CREAM margarine, sugar together. BEAT in eggs one at a time. MIX together flour, baking soda and salt. BEAT into creamed mixture. ADD vanilla. FOLD in sour cream and strawberries. POUR into oiled 9"x13" pan. BAKE 325 degrees 40 - 45 minutes or until center springs back when lightly touched.

ICING

1/2 cup	margarine
1/2 cup	cream cheese
2 cups	icing sugar
1 tsp.	vanilla

BEAT margarine, cream cheese, icing sugar and vanilla together until fluffy.

*Blueberries may be substituted for strawberries.

TRUDY'S PISTACHIO POUND CAKE

1 pkg.	white cake mix
1 pkg.	Pistachio flavor instant pudding
1/3 cup	oil
1 1/3 cup	water
3	eggs

BEAT all ingredients together for 3 - 5 minutes. POUR into oiled Bundt pan. BAKE 350 degrees 40 - 45 minutes or until toothpick inserted comes out clean. COOL for 10 minutes. REMOVE from pan and pour glaze over top.

GLAZE

1 cup icing sugar
1/2 tsp. almond extract
3 tbsp. milk

MIX icing sugar, almond extract and milk together until smooth. ADD more milk if necessary until it is of the desired consistency.

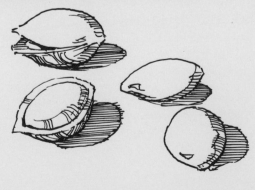

BREAD PUDDING

1 loaf	stale bread
4 cups	milk
3	eggs
1-1/2 cups	sugar
1 tsp.	nutmeg
1 tsp.	cinnamon
2 tbsp.	vanilla
1 cup	raisins

DICE the bread. POUR milk over it. Let stand 1/2 hour. BEAT eggs, sugar and vanilla together. STIR into bread mixture along with raisins. POUR into 9"x13" buttered baking dish. BAKE 325 degrees 1-1/4 hours.

WHISKEY SAUCE:

6 tbsp.	margarine
1 cup	sugar
1/2 tsp.	baking soda
1/2 cup	buttermilk
1/4 cup	whiskey or more if you prefer

MELT margarine. MIX in sugar, baking soda and buttermilk. COOK over low heat until mixture bubbles. REMOVE from heat. STIR in whiskey.

CUT pudding into squares. SPOON some whiskey sauce over individual servings.

Yield: 8 servings

PINEAPPLE DREAM

1/2 cup	orange marmalade
2 tbsp.	light corn syrup
1 tbsp.	brown sugar
2 cups	pineapple tidbits
1/4 cup	orange brandy
1 quart	vanilla ice cream

COMBINE and HEAT in saucepan marmalade, corn syrup and brown sugar stirring constantly. STIR in pineapple tidbits and brandy. HEAT thoroughly. SERVE warm over ice cream.

Yield: 6 servings

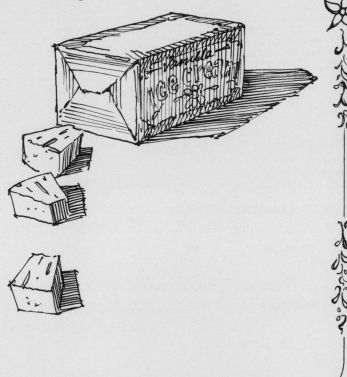

CLASSIC PUMPKIN PIE

1	9" uncooked pie shell, edges crimped high
1 1/2 cups	cooked pumpkin
3/4 cup	sugar
1/2 tsp.	salt
1 1/4 tsp.	cinnamon
1 tsp.	ground ginger
1/2 tsp.	nutmeg
1/2 tsp.	ground cloves
3	eggs slightly beaten
1 1/4 cup	milk
2/3 cup	evaporated milk

MIX together pumpkin, sugar, salt and spices. BLEND in eggs, milk and evaporated milk. POUR the filling into pastry shell. BAKE 400 degrees 50 minutes or until knife inserted in center comes out clean. COOL before serving.

THE ULTIMATE CHEESECAKE

3/4 cup	graham crumbs
3/4 cup	chopped walnuts
3 tbsp.	melted butter
2 lbs.	cream cheese
4	eggs
3	egg whites
1-1/2 cup	sugar
1 tbsp.	lemon juice
2 tsp.	vanilla

MIX together graham crumbs, chopped walnuts, and butter. PAT in bottom of 10" springform pan. BEAT cream cheese, eggs, egg whites, sugar, lemon juice, and vanilla until fluffy. POUR into pan. BAKE 350 degrees 1 hour. Turn off oven. Leave in partially open oven 1 hour. COOL in refrigerator overnight.

TOPPING:

2 cups	sour cream
1/4 cup	sugar
1 tsp.	vanilla

MIX together sour cream, sugar and vanilla. SPREAD over top of cheesecake. BAKE 350 degrees 10-15 minutes. REMOVE from oven. COOL. REMOVE from pan.

INDEX

INDEX

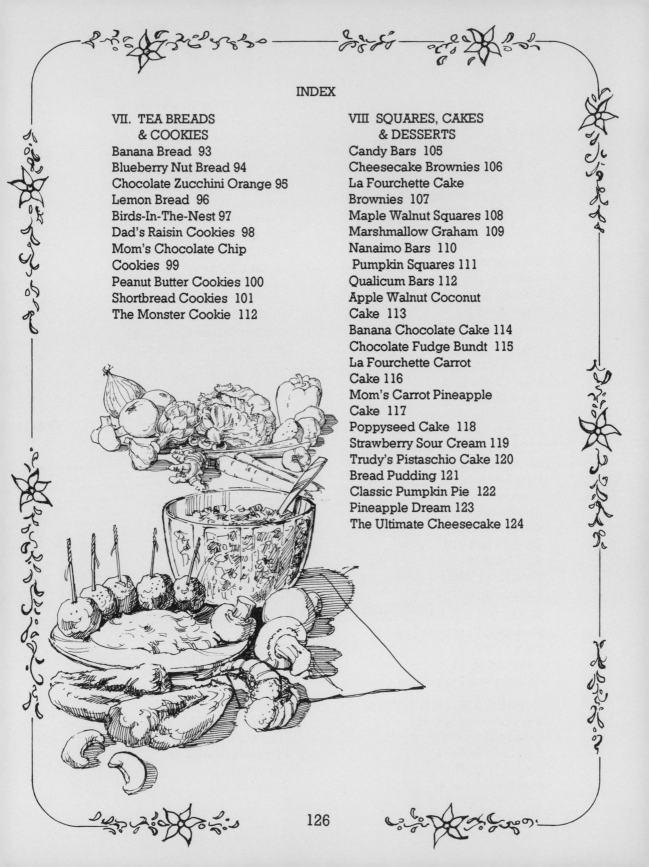

127